ZIMBABWE SPIN

POLITICS AND POETICS

Zimbabwe

- International boundary
- ‑ ‑ ‑ Province boundary
- ★ National capital
- ◉ Province capital
- Railroad
- Road

The cities of Bulawayo and Harare
have status equal to that of a province.

0   25   50   75 Kilometers
0   25   50   75 Miles
Lambert Conformal Conic Projection, SP 18.5/225

ZAMBIA

Lusaka

MOZAMBIQUE

NAMIBIA

BOTSWANA

MASHONALAND
CENTRAL

MASHONALAND
WEST

MASHONALAND
EAST

MATABELELAND
NORTH

MIDLANDS

MANICALAND

MASVINGO

MATABELELAND
SOUTH

SOUTH AFRICA

MOZAMBIQUE

MALAWI

Harare

Base 802836AI (C00254) 3-02

Reviews

Kathryn Waddell Takara's poems about Zimbabwe are political, lyrical, and thought pro-voking, describing great natural beauty. They contrast dire human poverty with soulful lessons of survival in a changing world. She is honest in her colorful, historical, and social observations.
—Daphne Barbee Wooten, Attorney, Author, Africanist

For any poet's "report" on anything, we must brace. Truth kicks and trickles in by surprise. Since her first visit in 2001 to Zimbabwe—formerly Rhodesia, named after 19th-century British mining tycoon Cecil John Rhodes—the poet has been growing memories and im-pressions of a nation held hostage by brutal dramatic legacies, colonial and post-colonial. Kathryn Takara admits: "I found myself between myth and reality, light and darkness, vulnerability and resilience." Wide-open and from such a ready heart, a shadow zone, she sides with the people always: "I became a golden arrow. / A quiver for your touch." She loves Zimbabwe, the very sound of it: "Let me be your waterfall / and then your joyous lake / let me come to you each day / a partnership we make." Stevie Wonder, among other Af-rican American entrepreneurs, invested big in Zimbabwe. On one country on the continent of her partial ancestry, poet-professor Takara lays down her lyric soul.
—Al Young, Former Poet Laureate of California

Kathryn Waddell Takara's latest collection of poetry is a redemption song for Zimbabwe. From colonialism to the country's struggle for freedom and its economic collapse, Takara follows the lives of the people as they fight for basic human rights yet continue to worship, dance, sing, love, and inspire us all by preserving their rich heritage and legacy. After these poems, in the words of Bob Marley, you will find out who the real revolutionaries are.
—Shelah Moody, Streetwise Radio, Island Stage Magazine

Kathryn Waddell Takara has captured the essence and emotional discovery of identity, compassion, and familiarity in *Zimbabwe Spin*. As she unravels the reality of Zimbabwe's political, economic, and sociocultural life, she reflects the visceral and dynamic life of this landlocked country, giving it the force and flow as powerful as the magnificent Zambezi River. With alliteration and fast-paced meter, Takara conveys the political reality of the country as well as her own roots in her poem, DIASPORA as she claims, "I, a black flower from the Pacific / a child of the beleaguered diaspora / seek regeneration / from your an-cient African sun." Takara draws pictures with lyrical words in ARCHEOLOGICAL DIG, providing a metaphorical compass that directs the reader to empathize and appreciate the striking truth of life in the Motherland. The historical lessons Takara shares in THE BEG-GAR: AFRICANS ARE ANCIENT provide the reader an authenticity of information that offers the present-day realism of Zimbabwe, reflecting the pragmatism that is at the very nature of the survival of African peoples.
—Tadia Rice, Author of *Transforming Horror into Hope: The Women of Rwanda*

OTHER BOOKS BY THIS AUTHOR

Love's Seasons: Generations Genetics Myths. Ka`a`awa, HI: Pacific Raven Press, 2014.

Timmy Turtle Teaches. Children's book. Ka`a`awa, HI: Pacific Raven Press, 2012.

Frank Marshall Davis: The Fire and the Phoenix (A Critical Biography). Ka`a`awa, HI: Pacific Raven Press, 2012.

Tourmalines: Beyond the Ebony Portal. Ka`a`awa, HI: Pacific Raven Press, 2010.

Pacific Raven: Hawai`i Poems. Ka`a`awa, HI: Pacific Raven Press, 2009. (Winner of 2010 American Book Award from the Before Columbus Foundation.)

New and Collected Poems. Berkeley, CA: Ishmael Reed Publishing, 2003.

Oral Histories of African Americans. Interviews by Kathryn Waddell Takara. Center for Oral History. Social Science Research Institute. Honolūlū, HI: University of Hawai`i at Mānoa, 1990.

CREDITS

"Archaeological Dig." *Love's Seasons: Generations Genetics Myths. Ka`a`awa, HI: Pacific Raven Press, 2014.*

"Zimbabwe VI," "Zimbabwe X," and "Mines and Hokey Pokey." *Julie Mango (Spring 2006).*

"Search," "Archeological Dig," "Zimbabwe Women," "Meltdown," "Drought," "Harare," "Strike," "Hardship," "Africans Are Ancient," and "Diaspora." *The African Journal of New Poetry: Beyond Subjectificatory Structures (2006).*

"Re-imagining African Literature." Essay. *Africa Literary Journal (2006).*

"In Harare," "Meltdown," "In Face of Hardship," "Drought," "Strike," "Zimbabwe Women," "Archeological Dig," "Africans Are Ancient," and "Diaspora." *Journal of African Literature and Culture: A Face from the Eye of Poetry (2006).*

"Zimbabwe Poems." *Konch (Summer 2001).*

"Zimbabwe." *Kaimana: Literary Arts Hawai`i (Spring 2001).*

ZIMBABWE SPIN

POLITICS AND POETICS

Kathryn Waddell Takara, PhD

Edited by Mera Moore

Pacific Raven Press

Ka`a`awa, Hawai`i

http://pacificravenpress.co

© 2015 by Kathryn Waddell Takara, Pacific Raven Press, LLC

Pacific Raven Press, LLC
Ka`a`awa, Hawai`i 96730

ISBN: 9 780986 075507

Front cover art by Larry Day

Back cover photograph by Joanne Lim

Photography by Kathryn Waddell Takara and Joanne Lim

Book Layout by Jonathan Zane, Eien Design **www.eiendesignstudio.com**

Cover design and concept by Kathryn Waddell Takara and Nancy Jones Karp

Editing by Mera Moore

This work is licensed under Pacific Raven Press, LLC.

Library of Congress Cataloging-in-publication data
Zimbabwe Spin: Politics and Poetics by Kathryn Waddell Takara, PhD

Catalogued as: Africana, African American, Poetry, Politics, Travel

Printed in the United States of America

Pacific Raven Press, LLC, is an independent publisher.
http://pacificravenpress.co/
pacificravenpress@yahoo.com

DEDICATION

To Karla and Asha

TABLE OF CONTENTS

LIST OF ILLUSTRATIONS

ACKNOWLEDGEMENTS

I am grateful to Divine Spirit, my ancestors, loving parents, husband Harvey Takara, and daughters Karla Brundage and Natasha Harrington for allowing me freedom through the years to dream, write, travel, and experience life and its many relations, permutations, mysteries, and adventures. I would be remiss if I did not also acknowledge my cherished family, the Waddell, Younge, Green, Braye, Calhoun, Wood, Valberg, and Takara clans, who loved, supported, and encouraged me.

Kudos to my teachers, from Tuskegee Chambliss Children's House and Tuskegee High School to the George School, from Tufts University to the University of Bordeaux, from the University of California at Berkeley to the University of Hawai`i at Mānoa—and to teachers of the Ouspensky/Gurdjieff schools and tradition of wisdom and consciousness— who gave me educational, creative, and philosophical foundations and helped me to grow in mindfulness, balance, scale, and vision.

I am ever grateful, even as the bird sings and affirms yes to the day, to my business manager and agent, Nancy Karp Jones, who kept me on task throughout the process, to my editor, Mera Moore, and to Jonathan Zane, graphics artist and designer extraordinaire!

I cannot forget to acknowledge my friends and neighbors from childhood to present, near, far, and deceased or disabled, who knew and know me, stood by and loved me, encouraged me to travel and spread my wings and words, and brought music and laughter, fruit, flowers and libations. I am indebted to those who read, listened to, and critiqued my fledgling verses and later finished works, who shared their time and space, ideas and feelings, philosophies and dreams, while we encouraged one another to keep our aims, supported each other in dismal times, and promoted our truths and understandings in the arts of communication, Diaspora studies, and political responsibility, including in no particular order, yet not limited to Paul Lyons, Peter Manicas, Miles and Bernice Jackson, Brenda Kwon, Rashidah Ismaili, George Gnopka, QR Hand, Ishmael Reed, Al Young, Barbara Christian, Opal Palmer Adisa, Frank Marshall Davis, Andre and Daphne Barbee Wooten, my Links sisters, Tadia Rice, Richard Hamasaki, Joe Balaz, `Imaikalani Kalahele and ohana, Libby Young, Tony Quagliano, Loretta Petrie, Allison Orr and Master Wang, the Carter ohana, Alison Frances, Elizabeth Buck, Andrea Anixt, Wendy Lagareta, Lani Lofgren, Carol Shepherd, Shelah Moody, Kathy Sloane, Amahra Hicks, Debbie and Mosso Ulii, the Thornton and Koff ohana, Reginald Lockett, Haunani-Kay Trask, Doug Matsuoka, Themba and Berita Khumalo, Julius Bagorette, Jay and Linda Hayden, Helen Matheus, Marty Conmy, Jeannine Lundgren, John Streetz, Gladys Crampton, Sharon and Tommy Yarbrough, Ernest Golden and others whom I have neglected to mention but who were there for me. Thank you!

I appreciate Nature for her glorious and magical speaking, the multiple aspects of the four elements, the organic dramas, and the powerful manifestations and mystical transformations. Nature is one of my greatest loves and teachers. She has taught me how to patiently observe and allow, to listen attentively, to humbly embrace and respect life, and to experience fully the senses. She embodies the mathematics of human nature and relations, relativity, planetary influences and the magnificent wonder of the Universe.
I am present, I am grateful, and I am blessed.

INTRODUCTION

Zimbabwe Spin

By Njoroge Njoroge, PhD, University of Hawai`i at Mānoa, Department of History

In these times of chaos we need, we must, have voices cast out to pull us back together. People do not seem to listen to each other anymore, they listen past, beyond, or simply ignore. And in this moment it is important, it is imperative, to listen together and draw connections that might not seem immediate. This is what makes the work and words of Kathryn Takara so powerful.

> Who sees, who listens
> who hears, who understands?

Takara's words force you to slow down, listen, learn, and think differently. These poems eloquently demonstrate the way the weight of the African past and the African present continue to inspire ongoing explorations of the self and our diasporic communities. At the end of the day it is all about the "work" of art, it is all about the voice, and it is all about an audience that is receptive and ready to listen to these truths.

Takara is able to convey and capture the spirit of a long, rich tradition of African diasporic language and spirituality. We hear over-tones and undertones of the oral tradition, African antecedents, the Black Arts Movement, and a rich blending of voices emerging from the colonies. Located in Hawai`i and traveling through Zimbabwe gives a particular resonance and movement to these writings. We are taken on journey at once foreign and domestic. We hear the sounds of the mine workers, the sorrows of our mothers, the anguish of a dream of liberation still deferred. At the same time we hear laughter, joy, hope, resistance and resilience. The poetics of a dream, that while deferred, refuses to surrender, refuses to die.

Takara is writing of and for Zimbabwe, channeling history, the legacies of imperialism, searching for meaningful forms of identification. Like the spider-writers of South Africa, these poems "of spidering voice," are prayers of protest and songs of defiance. Poetics and Politics, Politics and Poetics. We touch these with our lips as we read these words. "Where is home?" The question haunts the text, asking all of us to find our orientation "far from the familiar."

In these times of pain and danger we need words that help, words that heal, words that sing and spin and dance off the pages in our hands to the pages in our head to our actions in the world . . . the ways we "are and be" (an allusion to R&B music). The poet asks, "Were WE but an illusive dream?"

PROLOGUE

By Kathryn Waddell Takara, PhD

Zimbabwe! Former breadbasket of Southern Africa, referenced by musician Bob Marley in his song "98 Degrees in the Shade," has the potential to again become a prototype of accomplishment, achievement, and triumph for the peoples of Africa.

In January 2001, I visited my daughter in landlocked Zimbabwe for almost three weeks. My observations here focus on contemporary issues of the nation's freedom and identity amidst traditional values, mythologies, and history. Using poetry, I try to capture small slices of Southern African life and politics, specifically as seen briefly where I stayed in the Midlands between Harare and Bulayawo.

A brief political history sheds light on the fall of Zimbabwe, formerly known as Southern Rhodesia. The country was bypassed in the 1960s when many African countries declared their independence from colonial rule. Due to a stubborn settler regime, Zimbabwe was not able to declare independence until 1980, after a prolonged guerilla war. Problems arose among factions of Zimbabwean freedom fighters united against colonialism but divided in a struggle for governance and resources. During the era of dissent from 1982 to 1987, whole villages were burned by competing factions, with nearly 30,000 killed, often slaughtered, in brutal violent acts, including bayoneting pregnant women and throwing people into the deserted gold, copper, and mineral mines.

Eventually there was a unity accord. A policy of racial and ethnic reconciliation was inaugurated, which welcomed foreign and private investment, foreign embassies, NGOs, the World Bank, UNESCO, the Peace Corps, and a free press. The country soon thrived and became a prototype and model for the new independent African nations. Free elementary school education and health care were mandated, racial reconciliation was encouraged, and large infrastructure projects were undertaken.

A leader of the resistance movement, Robert Mugabe, belonging to the indigenous Eastern Shona ethnic group, was elected President in 1987, and for a while the country grew and thrived. And then came the disastrous fall. Initially committed to a Marxist/socialist agenda, Mugabe turned to North Korea for military training and for assistance in ridding the government of dissenters, mainly the Ndebele ethnic group from the Midlands to Bulawayo. Many peasants remained landless, underpaid, disenchanted, and disillusioned after the war for independence, with few visible changes in the quality of people's lives, in part because governmental policies advocated austerity for the poor.

By the late 1980s, radical changes began to occur with Mugabe's commitment to the redistribution of lands, perhaps in order to counter governmental scandals and blatant corruption. The intellectuals and students of the country became skeptical and restless as Mugabe moved away from socialism and wielded power with a heavy hand.

Demonstrations erupted. Small companies closed in favor of large corporations like Microsoft, unemployment grew, the economy declined, and the national debt increased. In the early 1990s, Mugabe married his secretary, who began to take huge sums of money out of the country to deposit in Europe, further depleting the national coffers.

By the late 1990s, the shortages and discontentment exploded. Factories closed; inflation became rampant; bankruptcies, protests, riots, and fuel shortages became normal; crime increased including robberies, credit-card fraud, and rapes; and famine closed in. The foreign banks pulled out, and loans were no longer available, which made the import of petroleum, fertilizer, and other essential raw materials almost impossible. Mugabe blamed whites. He accused the NGOs of subversive activities, political agendas, and interference in Zimbabwe's governance. He rejected established external services and projects for education, wells, dams, housing, agriculture, animal husbandry, and clothing.

In response to workers' needs and interests, unions gained strength and soon became restless and then angry with Mugabe's heavy-handed politics and intimidation practices. A new labor-based political party, the Movement for Democratic Change (MDC) led the opposition, with many Ndebele from the West helping in the resistance. The MDC had an open policy welcoming anyone who opposed Mugabe's party, the ZANU-PF. The MDC even included white commercial farmers, representatives of Western governments, NGOs, miscellaneous pressure groups, and local big businesses. As the national elections approached, a popular uprising led by the MDC threatened to defeat Mugabe, who went on the offensive by censoring and banning the media and disregarding numerous laws.

Mugabe sanctioned the growing intimidation, harassment, and violence instigated by the ZANU-PF against white farmers, calling for the confiscation of farmlands by black war veterans. He accused the MDC of siding with foreign interests and supported those who felt the white farmers should not be compensated for their confiscated lands. Since white-run farms and businesses had the seeds, fertilizer, and equipment essential to feed the nation, a slide into poverty and starvation ensued. Although land reforms were overdue, it was the leaders in his party who often benefitted from the confiscations. Furthermore, the people who settled on and took over the running of the farms often lacked the knowledge and tools to be productive.

Since then, especially as elections have approached, Mugabe has fostered a climate of chaos and terror toward the opposition. Zimbabwe continues to experience political unrest, economic crises, mass unemployment and crime rates, food and gas shortages, and a climate of fear as a result of Mugabe's administration. The sanctions from Western powers as well as an ongoing AIDS epidemic also dramatically slowed progress and development.

Mugabe, now 90 years old and president for over 30 years, was recently appointed chairman of the 54-nation African Union. He has promised to emphasize infrastructure, agriculture, and climate change. Time will tell if indeed these priorities are implemented.

But there is a positive side to Zimbabwe's history. The spiritual heritage, cultural wealth, and healing traditions unique to this region of Africa reveal the vibrant character and exemplary humor of the people. Zimbabwe is home to ecstatic healers and Victoria Falls, the ancient Great Wall and monastery of Zimbabwe, and famous sculptors and musicians. The game reserves, while significantly deteriorated and diminished, are still inspiring. The nation boasts a moderate climate where bananas and mangoes grow along with other fruits and vegetables. Until the turn of the 21st century, there was a well-developed infrastructure, an abundance of food grown for export, and many international investors.

During my brief sejour, I found myself between myth and reality, light and darkness, vulnerability and resilience. The values of an impartial divinity, family, friendship, peace, truthfulness, hard work, forgiveness, and reconciliation are supported by the ancient wisdom through perennial teachings of life's processes seen in the seasons, the ancestors, and proper relations found in art and folk tales. The nation's philosophy reveals the people's wit and cunning to assure their survival.

The people of Zimbabwe remain resilient, hardworking, and dignified. They possess a grace and joie de vivre which serves as a model for all humans: to return to laughter, to recover faith in the life process, to seek creative change, to enhance cultural identity through collective efforts and courage, to take risks in the name of survival yet always with a strong sense of conscience, and to maintain a sense of conscious community. Continually hopeful, the people are open to growth and new projects in conservation, farming, and irrigation. Intensely spiritual, they pray for oneness, valuing kindness, patience, diligence, and understanding, and they stoically believe that one day prosperity will return.

I

POLITICS

DIASPORA

Zimbabwe
I admire your longevity
your people's ebony hue
your open vistas welcoming each unknown new day.

Zimbabwe
I fear for you
your shrinking potentials
shriveled shortages of essentials
              water, power, petrol, condoms.

Zimbabwe
I hate your history
a bastard of colonial corruption
mismanagement deception
the undemocratic disfranchisement
of your powerless peasant people.

Zimbabwe
I love your beauty
jacaranda, frangipani, mangoes, mineral-rich earth
your round roofs covered with sturdy branches.

Zimbabwe
I respect your community
women working together
grinding wheat in deep wooden bowls
rhythms of preparing food and singing
even as strife, drought, and resistance
drain the productivity of your pastoral fields.

Zimbabwe
I, a black flower from the Pacific
a child of the beleaguered *diaspora*
seek regeneration
from your ancient African sun.

11/01/2014

4

SEARCH

Where are you
daughter mine
mixed-race woman
lost in a black sea of colonial remnants
where white people
and a few rich blacks
live behind 8-foot jagged walls
self-imprisoned
where Africans serve
or unemployed thousands wander by
under-trained or over-trained outsiders
looking for work.

Where are you
beautiful daughter mine
far away in Zimbabwe
where Americans and foreigners
are mistrusted
if not hated, feared
and paradoxically also admired.

How are you, daughter mine
with your daughter
my beautiful granddaughter
      acting up
      disagreeable
      disorderly
      disrespectful
blaming her mom and me
for her involuntary exile
in this ancient land
feeling banished
to an unsophisticated
isolated village
with a drain of wood shelf under the sky
for daily washed tea pot
deep sauce pan, stew pot
a few buckets and gourd containers
chipped enamel cups, bowls, plates.

When will I see both of you again?

ARCHEOLOGICAL DIG

Unearth fickle memory
Patterns of personal
Fragments of discarded histories
Ignored, forgotten, trampled
Abused resources environmental
Along dusty roads
Ancient in *Zimbabwe*.

Discover occasional diamonds of culture
Rare gems of parables, fabulous fables, perennial tales
Hidden knowledge
Dark mines of precious pleasures
Forgotten rituals, respect, and buried artifacts of nobility.

Decipher love songs and sacred ceremonies
Tucked away carefully, behind ebony masks
Deep in earlobes, under tongues, in throats
In secret treasure boxes hidden underneath the worn mattress of legacies
Familiar in the African *diaspora*.

Recover a beautiful tapestry of *Zimbabwe's* folded glory
Waterfalls, wild animals, cliff-side monasteries
Golden threads of revelations and a buried bottom of the Past.

Unveil conscious moments hidden in codes
Dig for laughter, dance, and traditions of family survival transcending millennia.

ZIMBABWE and *STRANGERS*

The *Great Zimbabwe*
The endless *Zambezi.*

Ancient friends forgotten
Buried in tribal weeds
Where once villagers gave honor and respect
To the spirits and ancestors
Held rituals and ceremonies
Respectful community traditions, familiar frontiers.

The *Great Zimbabwe*
The endless *Zambezi.*

One day
Strangers appeared like sudden winds
They appropriated the fertile land, precious metals, and gemstones
Creating confusion and chaos
Zimbabwe clear waters no longer available
Free fall
Into economic and political captivity.

The *Great Zimbabwe*
The endless *Zambezi.*

IN *HARARE*

The fancy hotel in *Harare*
boasts tea salons for the lodgers
old, blue-tiled swimming pools and darting red dragonflies
verdant gardens
adorned with life-sized stone sculptures
large lions, monkeys, and crocodiles artistically woven from wire
artificially lazing on the coiffed lawns.

Deferential waiters
serve loud and rude *Rhodies* at the fancy hotel
who remember with nostalgia
the safaris and killing wild animals
the grand *Rhodesia* before independence
where Western "civilization" and order reigned
and natives knew their place.

Nowadays it is hard to ignore
the sullen *Shona,* the hungry *Ndebele*
hard to forget
the ignoble history of colonial wars
of *Shaka Zulu* and veranda cultures
where animal skins, heads, and various horns
hang on the walls, a testimonial art.

War veterans and descendants thrive, still alive
in the reserves, in the homesteads, around *Bulawayo.*

Meanwhile
tourists are dwindling
money is devalued
inflation and fear are real and rampant.

Occasional African guests arrive
and assume their place at the table
the facade of elegance continues
at the fancy hotel
under a bright cobalt blare of sun.

The *Rhodies* complain, get white drunk and abusive
to the waiters who serve and listen patiently
jaws clenched
tensions jumping
in facial veins
underneath their black, black skins.

MELTDOWN

Under the rule of a zealot
Opponents beaten and discouraged
Thwarted elections
Forgotten revolution
The meaning of democracy.

Wild animals near extinction
Illegal hunters
Heedless, greedy poachers
Elephants and rhinos at high risk
Endangered even on animal preserves
Rare tusks for ancient Chinese remedies
Jewelry, decorative art, piano keys
Where empty nests dot the abandoned trees in leafless intricacy
All Nature a sunset witness.

Ignorant collaborators
Hungry, envious of Western wealth
Commit unspeakable acts of cruelty to feed their families and greed.

Awesome independence corrupts
Distorted collective vision of progress
Ignores economic meltdown
As policy supports political intimidation
Social unrest dominated by bully tactics.

Like magma inflates before an eruption
Discontent rumbles under the volcano of political inequality.

STRIKE

Whispers of trouble
striking workers in *Harare*
once called *Salisbury*
home where *Doris Lessing* wrote
Children of Violence
of friends falsely gay
where the old white oligarchy
dines with dysfunctional families
and small circles of friends.

Rhodies create their own mythology
as savior sojourners
still unaware of the *Great Zimbabwe*
the ancient kingdoms
dismiss the fall to suffering
of a dispossessed people
feel guiltless for shameless theft of a once-rich nation.

IN THE FACE OF HARDSHIP

Drought in the *Midlands*
dirty water turned off during the night
tax levies
farm occupations
terrorism by *war veterans*
and political activists
        sanctioned by the authorities.

Mismanagement
downsizing
economic collapse
poverty
malaria
rapes
murder
car-jackings
purse snatchings
pathetic prisons
political prisoners
HIV orphans
        broken families.

In face of hardship
many still smile
work
believe
hope
marry
procreate
for the next generation
        singing freedom.

THE BEGGAR: AFRICANS ARE ANCIENT

I

Please madam, I am hungry
please madam
again
please, buy this carved zebra.

Africans
are ancient
people
civilization continent
incomprehensible
old as diamonds, dinosaurs, apes
pyramids and perfumes
unknown as volcanoes.

Sunlight dances on black skin
laughter rings
clear as a new day
intense as burning fires
extremities tested
alchemy around
abounds.

A way of life ripples
across the planet
dance and breath
familiar like drums
jazz in movement
spontaneous
full of ancient and deliberate themes.

II

Please madam, I am hungry
please madam, I carved this fine
zebra
again
please, take this one.

Neo-colonial paradigms
promote imbalance.

Sneers flit across faces
of otherwise kind people.
Fathers imagine power.
Exploitation consciousness
breeds cold lives in false
competition and treachery to survive.

In an ancient land, self-righteous blunders and
abuse continue.
Those blinded by greed
hold no respect
for responsible goodness
for ancient hierarchies
for community.

III

Down the street
tawdry youth implore
beseech, follow, reach out
grab, pull.l.l.lllll....

Please madam, I am hungry
please madam
again please, see how heavy he is
my zebra
madam
please, the soapstone is number 1 quality
please
please, is cheap for you.

Please I am hungry
we are hungry
you are not
hungry
maybe I will kill
the elephants and rhinos
at the watering hole at dusk
so I can eat.

IV

Legacy of colonial
lacks cooperation
lacks respect for Africans
no threads of compassion connect
the difference, the chasm
the almost void
of understanding
each other (the Other) humans
Hu, you, who man
Hu chant to enlightenment.

We see.

Colonial procedures require
free labor for trade
dehumanization for profits
to satisfy power's desires
for comfort and ease.

V

Progress inequitable
the legacy remains.

Please madam, I am hungry
I give you good price.
Buy my carved zebra.

Poor Africans
work the mines
extract the diamonds, gold, oil
poach for ivory
kill the animals
for others far away
dreams of exotic potions and notions
the balance of nature at a precipice.

Disease follows drought
unemployment, hunger
transference of people
values, communities
disruptions, destruction
as thousands die daily.

Separated families
hunger growls
like the lions on the *veld*
treacherous conditions
whether working in the mines
or laboring in private homes.

VI

Africans grew consciousness
of exploitation, deprivation
organized labor
strikes, fights, demonstrations
for electoral change of policy.

Aspiring voters monitored closely
by the ruling party
elections interrupted, postponed results
altered, manipulated.

The West judges *Zimbabwe*
with harsh sanctions
for its corrupt procedures
in a sham democracy.

But Africa is an ancient land
regularly ravaged
predictably surviving
as her sensibilities and strengths
sustain.

Creative melodies of possibility
flash across the darkening horizon
like dry lighting above evening fires.

Please, please madam. Please.

DROUGHT

Slaves of the climate
whirl through red and orange feelings
surrounded by dry stars in an ebony night.

Thirsty emotions unleashed
gallop out of control
to an unknown horizon of lack.

A drought of absence and access
falls breathlessly to the dusty earth.

People pray for rain.

NEWSPAPER: HELP WANTED

I
Accounting degree minimum
Articulate
Very presentable
International exposure an added advantage
Required to take care of demanding customers
And ensure their delight
Preferably no experience.

II
Literacy essential
Good health
Well-groomed
Serious demeanor
Ability to work under pressure
Without supervision
Active in sports or martial arts
Willing to do anything
As a guide for Executive Tourists.

III
Need 20 untrained guards
Tall under-covers
We are masters in training
Guarantee top security placement.

IV
Require someone
Prepared to travel regularly
To Mozambique across troublesome border with land mines
Good communication skills essential
        in English and Portuguese
Sympathetic to Christian aims
Understanding of HIV/AIDS and development issues
Ability to communicate with stakeholders
Orphans and other affected parties
And easily adaptable.

BROKEN FAMILIES

Fathers absent
work in cities
disillusioned by poor wages
drink frustrations
suffer lays-offs, slow-downs
duped by city slickers and corrupt morals.

Mothers and children in the homesteads
maintain the standard four huts
work parched fields
misery, drudgery, hunger
jealousy, envy, inadequate health facilities
misunderstandings multiplied.

Single mothers in cities
outcasts, addicts, diseased, barren.

Broken families tug at heartbeats
fragile, almost defeated
by demons of privilege
white skins.

Spirits of the dead
hover near the sacred tree
shake branches
rattle dry grass
compel attention
call call call the hungry ones
to wake up
remember ancient mysteries
resist the would-be conquerors.

Who sees, who listens
who hears, who understands?

ZIMBABWE WOMEN

Passionate women

Laughing, crying
Working, playing
Walking, carrying
Singing, cooking
Birthing, grieving
Nursing, teaching
Cleaning, planting
Building, harvesting
Stubborn, enduring

Sustained intensity
Zimbabwe women
Not to be subdued.

MINES AND HOKEY POKEY

Mines, land grabs
undercurrents of unease and fear
psychological physical handicaps.

Age-o
day oh
shake it to the North, South
up and down like sex.

Toys and joys
burdens of possession
responsibilities permanent
grown up until you drop dead
permanent and blatant
like mountains
burdensome on the path
of freedom's gate.

Dancing, laughter
shake it to the east
invocation to the sun
shake it to the west
companion to the night
Zimbabwe cows, milk shakes
unpasteurized experience
brought back to the gratitude of family life.

Shake it round
shekere
best is rest
dance of presence at sunset and cooking fires
to harvest in applause and light
after the drumming performance.

Husbands absent and working the mines
night stars moving planets
wives strong, face darkness without fear.

ELEPHANTS ON BLUE CLOTH
(Reflections on a Cotton *Pagne, Mandela,* and America in Crisis)

I

9/11/01
911 - Calling 911

A question of freedom
Spirit of change after the
three-pronged attack
Trade center buildings down
3,000 dead
Al Qaeda surprise.
Time to seek security
comfort in family.

I miss you, my daughter
this cerulean morning
even as the nation and world grieve
at America's new war
The planes are flying near empty
war ships, troops and aircraft
on the move
like large elephants
toward strategic locations.

I hum a *Hu* chant
of healing and love
for family and friends of trapped
spirits wailing in cavernous blue
toxic fumes.
I wish you were near.

Tragedy of *9/11*
shock of fire
and twisted metal
political analysis, personal reaction
replayed to numbness on TV
fires of hysterical unity
smoldering in arrogance
missiles pointed presidentially
to defend this land of illusive
freedom.

II

I was walking toward the seashore
wearing my blue *pagne*
bought in *Kwe Kwe*
printed with elephants
carrying the memory of music
and markets shared
strumming love for you.

Then I heard the news
turned back shocked
an urgency in my solar plexus
to write.
You landlocked in *Zimbabwe*
me on a remote island chain
on the other side
of the planet and equator
surrounded by the blue Pacific
still in an altered state of shock
this first day of fall 2001.

III

911, Emergency, Emergency!
September 11, 2001
America staggers under an attack
on our illusion of unconquerable
material symbols, secure fortresses boundaries,
weaponry
global trade, stock market
airlines and travel industry
businesses and leisures
of complacent middle America
cushioned from war and
unpredictable suffering
all brought to a screeching halt
in a matter of melting minutes.

The privileged of the planet stunned
no longer surrounded
with comfort and ease
cell-phone gossip unavailable to all.

In New York City
the fall of the twin towers
the horror of flames
people flinging themselves
falling 85 floors to their deaths
families, friends, colleagues
suddenly irrevocably separated.

IV

I remember bright banana mornings
Erzulie shimmering on ocean
comfortable like today
when intimacy and peace of mind
was refreshing and accessible
as the sea down the road
when communication was reliable
and compromise assumed.

I recollect Western history
others wailing for centuries
barely daring to openly critique
American indifference, superiority
while power grew and prospered
but at whose expense and sacrifice
certainly not only our own.

My thoughts return to *Zimbabwe*
where my daughter now resides.
Ancient people lived peacefully
before the horrors of colonialism
black souls laughing under the sun
surviving with dignity in Nature.

I imagine souls sharing with others
even in times of scarcity
sometimes complaining
when hungry or ill
not resorting to mindless slaughter
and destruction of innocents
simple folk striving to have enough
for the cycles of birth and growth
elders' consciences responsible
and respected by sturdy youth
wisdom of generations passed along.

V

But now, *9/11/01*
911 - Calling 911

A siren wails discord
survival is an issue
poverty becomes a red flag
AIDS, racism
theft of oil and precious resources
can no longer be ignored
air, earth, fire, water
elemental survival, pure peace
no longer assured or assumed
humans at risk.

I miss you today too far away
even as the paternal bully
of national imperialism is humbled
when faced with a spiraling cliff
of violence and economic disaster
the powerful allies of fear.

Patriotism potentially irrational
thunders
across the plains of technology
homeland security
wiretaps, searches, pat downs
transformed travel and transportation.

Momentarily I fear
for the survival of our love and life
the familiar traditions
of the old world.
I imagine the loss
of our extravagant ease
the luxury of entertainment
the fabric of our humanity.
I remember *Doris Lessing's*
apocalyptic visions of scarcity.

VI

But listen, a gong reverberates
behind the immobile mountains.
A global peace movement gathers
to remind of authenticity and love
values of deliberation and democracy
seeking strategies of compromise
balance, communication reconciliation.

Self-reflection no longer
can be ignored.
We are all guilty.

It is time to observe our own
behavior patterns
the movement of relations
up and down the spiral of allowing
lessons to be learned.
Righteousness falls to ego
which rises with a conquering sword.

Daughter, the dog whines
for attention, barks at the cat
who keeps a respectful distance between them.
They do not kill one another.

Where is the observing bald eagle
ancient, sacred metaphor of insight perched on the highest nest?
The bird's splendid discernment
to be shared with all.
Who will see?

From on high is there a collective vision of balanced healing?
A *mandala* of blue design?
Can the elephants and rhinos survive?
Where are *Mandela* and *King*?
Can we change how we react?

9/11/01
911 - Calling *911*

II

POETICS

FORGOTTEN GLORY

Zimbabwe!
I celebrate the atlas of your body
antipode of *Hawai`i*
landlocked and sun parched.

I sing your forgotten glory
lions and monkeys now woven in wire
ancient earth, timeless people
remembered in *Shona* songs
in *Ndebele* clicks and kisses
under star-flung nights.

I celebrate you
with a poem of spidering verse
on and off the cold wall of separation
transcending fears of retribution
under a blazing sun.

DEAR *ZIMBABWE*

I was alone in a dark tunnel
When you came and forged me with your spirit.

You made the dawn leap
Offering a horizon of inspiration.

I became a golden arrow
A quiver for your touch.

In the silence of the morning
A double rainbow arced across your sky.

ZHOMBE

Even in the middle of 10 acres of maize

Even under a scorched *Zimbabwe* azure
sky leaning into the mirage of day

Zhombe is an oasis
music in laughter, walking, talking.

Can one dance the drought away?

Even in the center of *Zimbabwe Midlands*
my soul crescendos for the place I love.

ILLUSIVE INTIMACY

Illusive as three stars
sandwiched between a virgin vulva of clouds
soon to be erased

Moonlight on bare arms
evening mists cooling passion
a shooting star
a middle-aged wish
for flashes of ecstasy
never to be fulfilled

Memory of *Zimbabwe*
clarity marred by concealed forces
distant lightning portends danger
spies behind walls
uneasiness of unfamiliar steps
heard in the darkness
slippery political intrigue

Movement in the intimate sky
parallels spheres of shifting desires and influences.

LANDLOCKED: JOYOUS LAKE

Let me be your water
a pool to slake your thirst.
Let me be your nurse
to bring you strength and truth.

Let me bring you gentleness
to mend your stressful day.
Let me touch your hurts and wounds
and heal them through the night.

Let me listen to your sounds
be moved by your sweet tunes.
Let me write you poems of love
and conjure stars and moon.

Let me be your waterfall
and then your joyous lake.
Let me come to you each way
a partnership we make.

FIRE AND GRACE

You filled me with fire
even in the coldest of emotional nights

You brought out my sun
even in the roots of my loneliness

You gave birth to my soul
even as the trees and birds slept

The bright stars
witnessed the grace of your creation.

RED DRAGONFLIES

Around the swimming pools
at the hotel in Harare

Iridescent ruby dragonflies dance and dart happily
with Zimbabwean choreography in the air

Vermillion melodies invade my heart and body
when highlife presence leaves no place for sadness
and missing you.

ZIMBABWE FIRES

I

A day without you
is like fire on the *savanna*
no water in sight in the dry season.

I come to you on the *veld*
you chase me away.
You run.
I go
elusive as a wind fairy.
Red, orange, saffron hours
singe my brown hands, legs, neck.
Strong medicine
is the realm of physical.

Shimmering, shining, smiling
your bright light tingles too hot
time too short
ladder of hours, minutes
days, weeks, months, memories.

II

The wind picks up on the *veld*.
Smoke dances unpredictable
as syncopated emotions.
The people can see
around the evening fires
send receive and understand
distant drum signals.

On the high plains
people light fires and cook
anytime, on the dry sides
of the road to anywhere
roasting something anything
eating tangy, spicy, blackened
iodine in insects
black *mopani* worms
iron from freshly slaughtered
roasted meat.
Calcium from goat's milk
grows strong white teeth.

All around, day and night
fires dance like jazz
do not bite
even the women
in their long wrapped *pagnes*
making and tending the fires
talking and cooking
sipping water
from a communal bucket
questionable standards
of Western purity
to quench
the ever-present lingering thirst.

Children run by
Too close to the fires.
Sparks fly in the poltergeist wind
laughter all around.

III

Even in the smoke
you are everywhere
with me in my dreams.
You run across my memory
as I sit waiting by the cooking fire
for you to return and be at my side.

I return to hope
security and conjugal feeling.
I sit in anticipation
silent, sure, and still
my heart not jumping, crackling
whooshing with fiery emotions.

I wait late by the cold embers
but you do not return.

You are gone like the smoke.
The daylight of my hope sags
droops in a night of sorrow
still longing for your tingling touch
your notes of firing intensity
your absent rhythms.

IV

The talking drums beat loudly
a message from a raging fire of love
I follow the rhythmic sounds
down the dark distance
only to discover cold huts
wailing women
short-haired girls, lean hungry boys
slowly dying of deprivation
while unemployed men stoically hold back their solitary tears
fiery hearts spinning out of control.

MORNING MEMORY

I remember you
as you were that morning in a traditional hut
near the *Zambezi*.
Your hair shimmered
in the golden sun.
You gave me a loving surprise.
Your tingling kisses fell all over me
intimate as lingering starlight at soft dawn.

WHERE IS HOME?

Laughing in the moment with you
near or far away from familiar
happy as the bright *Zhombe* sun
in the highlands of *Zimbabwe* near *Kwe Kwe.*

SMALL HIKE

No longer welcome at the edge of green
before the drought and ghosts of sensations.

Ancestral trees and experiences
seem inconsequential on the side of the narrow path.

A distant precipitous mountain looms indigo
yet to be climbed.

Truncated turquoise moments
invisibly pass along my imagination
over swinging hand bridges of mystery
near the thundering *Victoria Falls.*

I pause in presence
your unpredictable absence noticed
a spectral haunting like the mists around the falls
leaving traces of real on the passage.

I feel a bottomless lack as fading memory
sinks and drowns under an indifferent *Zimbabwe* sky.

UNDER A *ZHOMBE* MOON

Your touch is like a *Zimbabwe* dance
lively, quick, rhythmic.

Your words are like a rare clear pool
quiet, still, soothing.

Your body is like the music
rippling, magnetic, strong.

Where did you go?
Were WE but an imagined dream
under a *Zhombe* moon?

ZIMBABWE SPIN

Golden ambrosia
young collaboration
communication once more
adaptation
in the light of the shimmering *bani.*

Springtime spins
you, me, we witness
pale yellow light on morning leaves
clear as new love
green as *Zimbabwe* after the torrential rainy season.

I dance and listen to the rhythms of inspiration's freedom
empty space like a new page
waiting to birth an enchanting vision.

I focus once again on the possibilities of emptiness
woven like a tapestry
half real, half imagined
creative even in your drumming absence.

Sudden as an intercepting jet
I am attacked by a feeling of being trapped
squeezed to act under a spotlight of pressure
controlled by an unfamiliar outer force of land-lock
infected by blocked feelings, no longer able to see or hear clearly.

I remember *Zimbabwe*
where people laugh and weep freely
life jumps out, whirls, spins
even in the face of daily deaths and viruses of dysfunction
unreliable electricity and dirty water
even when floods, drought, and censorship
threaten freedom's survival.

I am inspired to return to Mother *Zimbabwe*
to go, find you, and giggle together under a full moon
whirl deliriously in *Midlands* darkness
spin singing under a star-flung *Zimbabwe* night.

RESCUE MISSION

Consider the past.
Consider the dream.
Consider the missed mark.

Who will rescue
Zimbabwe?

Who can choose to decide
freedom?

Who will alter an essence
of egotistical power?

Who can see, listen
and turn toward objective wisdom?

Who will excavate the treasures
of sacred self?

Who can pay attention
who can learn?

Z

zip, zing, sing
Zimbabwe

far from *Zaire*
zoom, *zezazz*
zig zag down to the *Zambezi*
to see the zebras by the river
wear the zoris or
zounds! watch out for big mambas

zip, zing, sing
Zimbabwe

zap the mosquitoes
get zany not zealous like *Mugabe*
zone out on the zodiac
zowie! the stars blaze bright in a country with few lights
the thorn *zarebas* protect the farmers and harvest
from the hungry lions

zip, zing, sing
Zimbabwe

find traces of the *Zulu*
not tourist zombies at the zoo
stake a plot of land, walk on the veld
grow corn and zucchini
make *zaffer* glaze of cobalt for the pottery
on the shelf in the traditional hut

zip, zing, sing
Zimbabwe

meanwhile
twin jets streak across cloudless infinity of empty aqua sky
create temporary white lines of parallel being
zap! while consciousness moves and disappears
a dancing moment of exquisite stillness in *Zimbabwe* moments

zip, zing, sing
Zimbabwe

GLOSSARY

Words that appear in this glossary are italicized in the poems to assist the readers.

bani - Used in Eckankar spiritual practice, it means "shimmering light to heaven."

Bulawayo - The second-largest city in **Zimbabwe** after the capital city, Harare. The city is located in the region of Matabeleland, six-to-seven hours by car southwest of Harare.

Children of Violence - See **Lessing**.

diaspora - Refers to a large group of people, who share a similar heritage or homeland, dispersed and spreading their culture across the world. The term originates in an ancient Greek word meaning "to scatter" or "to spread about." The word generally describes large migrations of refugees, languages, or cultures.

Erzulie (also spelled Erzili and Ezili) - A goddess of love, the female energy of the African deity Legba. Of Nigerian origin and particularly revered in Haiti, Erzulie is both feared and adored. She represents language, love, help, goodwill, health, beauty, and fortune, as well as jealousy, vengeance, and discord. She is symbolized by the image of a coiled serpent.

frangipani - The plumeria plant, with fragrant white and yellow flowers. Native to Latin America and the Caribbean, it can grow in tropical or subtropical regions.

Great Zimbabwe - An anthropological stone ruin that is a UNESCO World Heritage Site located in the mountains of Southeastern Zimbabwe near the city of Masvingo and Lake Mutirikwe. In Africa, the term "Great" distinguishes larger archaeological sites from smaller ones. It is generally agreed that, in the 4th to 7th centuries, the Gokomere people (ancestors of today's Shona people) populated the area. Between the 9th and 15th centuries, they erected three subsequent cities in different areas, surrounding each with stone walls. The site served as the capital of the Kingdom of Zimbabwe from 1220 to 1440 and was a major trading center. The first Westerner to report on the site was a Portuguese sea captain, Vincente Pegado, in 1531. The British began excavating the site in 1870. Westerners spread many inaccurate rumors about the origins of the site, including the discounted claim that it was the capital of the Biblical Queen of Sheba.

Harare (called Salisbury from 1890 until 1982) - The capital city and the leading metropolitan province of Zimbabwe. Located in the northeast in a region known as Mashonaland, it has an estimated population of 2.5 million. Two years after Zimbabwean independence from British colonial occupation, it was renamed Harare. Its economy is based on the mining of diamonds, gold, and other rare minerals, manufacturing of steel and chemicals, and trade.

Hawai`i - A collection of islands in the Pacific ocean. Originally an independent kingdom, in 1895, a group of white missionary descendants and business leaders overthrew the indigenous monarchy with the assistance of U.S. marines. Since 1949, the islands have been the 50th state of the United States.

highlife - An African music genre that originated in Ghana at the beginning of the 1900s and spread throughout West Africa. The up-tempo sound is produced by, among other instruments, multiple guitars and jazzy horns.

Hu - Certain mantras or chants used to facilitate spiritual growth in the spiritual practices of Eckankar and other various mystical traditions. ECKists sing Hu alone or in groups, believing that singing Hu draws the soul closer in a state of consciousness to the Divine Being. Eckankar is a non-denominational religious movement founded in the U.S. in 1965 by Paul Twitchell, who was the first Mahanta, or Living ECK Master, followed by Darwin Gross and then Harold Klemp. More information about Eckankar can be found at www.eckankar.org.

jacaranda - Flowering plant that has been introduced to nearly every tropical and subtropical region in the world. It is often blue or purple in color.

King, Martin Luther, Jr. (1929-1968) - A minister and a leader of the U.S. African American Civil Rights Movement. Born in Georgia, he earned a bachelor's degree in sociology from Morehouse College in 1948, a bachelor's degree in divinity from Crozer Theological Seminary in 1951, and a doctoral degree in systematic theology from Boston University in 1955. He became a Baptist pastor in 1954. He was a leader of the Montgomery Bus Boycott of 1955 and many subsequent direct actions against segregation. After his arrests for participating in a civil-rights march, he wrote his famous 1963 piece titled "Letter from Birmingham Jail," which enumerates the reasons protesters must continue to fight against the injustice of segregation laws. He delivered the keynote speech at the March in Washington, DC, in 1963, and won the Novel Peace Prize in 1964. He continued fighting for civil rights, voting rights, and equal rights in housing. Toward the end of his life, he spoke against the Vietnam War and against poverty. He was assassinated in 1968.

Kwe Kwe - A city located in Midlands Province in the center of Zimbabwe, roughly equidistant between the cities of Harare and Bulawayo. The city has a population of about 100,900. It is known for producing steel and fertilizer.

Lessing, Doris May (1919-2013) - Author of fiction, poetry, plays, librettos, and biographies. Born to British parents in Persia (now Iran), she was raised in Southern Rhodesia (now Zimbabwe). Her novels include *The Grass Is Singing*, five novels collectively titled *Children of Violence, The Golden Notebook, The Good Terrorist,* and five novels jointly known as *Canopus in Argos: Archives.* When awarded the 2007 Nobel Prize in Literature, she was described by the Nobel committee as "that epicist of the female experience, who with skepticism, fire, and visionary power has subjected a divided civilization to scrutiny." She was an early feminist and also a mystic.

malaria - Mosquito-borne infectious disease of humans and other animals caused by a parasitic microorganism. Malaria causes headache, fever, fatigue, and vomiting, and in serious cases yellow skin, seizures, coma, and death. If not treated appropriately, symptoms can recur. Resistance immunity is temporary.

mamba - Fast-moving, venomous terrestrial snake, sometimes called a tree asp, which is native to Africa. Related to the cobra, the mamba exhibits a similar threat display by stretching and opening its mouth. Humans are their main predators. These snakes generally avoid contact with humans.

mandala - From Sanskrit, a circular spiritual and ritual symbol in Hinduism and Buddhism, representing the universe. Often inside the circle are four T-shaped gates, each containing another circle with a center point. The symbol is used in meditation as a tool for focusing attention and establishing a sacred space.

Mandela, Nelson Rolihlahla (1918-2013) - President of South Africa from 1994 to 1999, after a long imprisonment for his commitment to liberation of his nation. Born into the Thembu royal family of the Xhosa people, from his elders he learned African history and traditions. Prohibited from being educated with whites, he attended all-black schools and colleges, and he finished his bachelor's degree via a correspondence course with the University of South Africa in 1943. Studying law at the University of Witwatersrand in Johannesburg, as its first black student, he experienced racism. In 1944, he helped found the African National Congress Youth League (ANC), which undertook protests and actions against the white domination known as apartheid. In 1953, he passed his law exams and became an attorney. In 1956, the South African government arrested him for high treason, and the trial dragged on. In 1959, led by a new black liberation group, the Pan-African Congress (PAC), blacks began burning the passes that whites forced them to carry. The government declared martial law. According to the African Studies Center of Michigan State University, in "South Africa: Overcoming Apartheid," 3.5 million non-whites were forcibly moved to segregated areas between 1960 and 1983. In 1960, after burning his pass, Mandela was again arrested, and the ANC and PAC banned, but in 1961 the new charges against him were dropped and he was found not guilty of earlier charges. He and others continued leading the opposition to apartheid, agreeing to support violent sabotage so long as there was no loss of life. He traveled to nations in Africa and Europe seeking support for the anti-apartheid movement, and he briefly studied guerrilla warfare. In 1962, he was arrested and sentenced to five years, and the government pursued even more charges against him. In 1964, he was sentenced to life in prison. He and other black leaders suffered in prison. It took until the late 1980s for pressure inside and outside of South Africa to bring about the defeat of apartheid. Mandela was released in 1990, and the ANC negotiated with the government to end apartheid and hold elections. In 1994, the newly elected National Assembly chose him as the nation's first black president. He and his government worked to reduce racial inequality, institutionalized racism, and poverty; it also promoted formal processes for racial reconciliation.

Midlands - A province of Zimbabwe, located in the center of the nation. With a population of about 1.6 million, it contains people from the Shona, Ndebele, Tswana, Suthu, and Chewa ethnic groups. The province's capital, Gweru, is the nation's third-largest city. Another major city of the Midlands is Kwe Kwe.

mopani - A species of moth found in Southern Africa. Tasty and nutritious, the moth's large edible caterpillar, known as the *mopani* worm, is a major protein source for indigenous Southern Africans. In Zimbabwe, the worms are a staple in rural areas and considered a delicacy in the cities. The worms can be dried and enjoyed for their crunchiness, like potato chips. They can also be eaten after cooking them so that they retain their plumpness, and drenching them in sauce.

Movement for Democratic Change (MDP) - See **Mugabe**.

Mugabe, Robert Gabriel (1924-) - A revolutionary against British colonial rule who became a politician, and the President of Zimbabwe since 1987. He is a member of the Shona ethnic group. Although as a black, he would have been prevented from achieving a significant level of education, as a boy he was educated by Jesuits. He demonstrated a voracious appetite for learning and earned numerous university degrees including two law degrees. He worked as a teacher from 1955 to 1960. A leader of one of the many rebel groups struggling against white minority rule, he was imprisoned for a decade from 1964 to 1974, continuing his rebel activities after his release. Since 1975, he has led the Zimbabwe African National Union-Patriotic Front party (ZANU-PF). The party formed as a union of two prior rebel groups, Mugabe's ZANU aided by the Chinese and Joshua Nkomo's Zambia-based ZAPU supported by the Soviets. When ZANU-PF won the 1980 parliamentary elections, Nkomo's faction was left with influence only in the Matabeleland provinces. In 1980, Mugabe was chosen prime minister, holding that office until 1987, when he became the nation's first president, with broad powers. ZANU-PF maintained a majority in parliament until 2008, when the Movement for Democratic Change party (MDP) won a majority of seats, and ZANU-PF had to grant concessions to them. The MDP had formed in 1999 in opposition to ZANU-PF. The MDC originated with a broad coalition of individuals, civic groups, and labor unions campaigning for a "No" vote in the 2000 constitutional referendum. After the 2005 elections, the party split into two factions, which reunited in 2008 after winning a combined majority in parliament. The MDP remains the main opposition party to ZANU-PF. In the 2013 elections, ZANU-PF regained its control over parliament, winning two-thirds of the seats. Mugabe has been reelected president seven times despite accusations of fraud, vote-rigging, and intimidation. His leadership has been marked by accusations of engaging in brutality, running a police state, and ruining Zimbabwe's economy. (See the Introduction to this book for further information about Mugabe.)

Ndebele - An ethnic group belonging to the Bantu peoples in Southern Africa, who share a common Ndebele culture and language. In the early 19th century, a Zulu Chief named Mzilikazi split from King Shaka. Absorbing other clans, the Zulu he led eventually controlled the area known today as the Southern Ndebele.

911 - The telephone number one calls in the U.S. and Canada to reach police, fire, ambulance, and other emergency services.

9/11 (also 9/11/01, September 11th, September 11, 2001) - The date on which nineteen male al-Qaeda operatives conducted four airplane highjackings as a coordinated terrorist attack on the U.S. After leaving Massachusetts' Boston International Airport, two of the planes crashed into the twin World Trade Center towers in New York City. The plane from

Virginia's Dulles International Airport crashed into the Pentagon in Washington, DC. Passengers on the plane that had left New Jersey's Newark International Airport heard about the attacks and fought with the highjackers; the plane crashed in a field in Shanksville, Pennsylvania. In the attacks, 2,977 victims and 19 highjackers were killed. The victims included 2,646 Americans and 372 people who were citizens from over ninety other nations around the world.

pagne - A long rectangular piece of cloth, often brightly colored or decorated, worn by women in Africa. It is tightly wrapped around the torso and tucked at one corner with the ends falling free. It can be worn as a dress, skirt, or undergarment, and depending on the fabric can be worn for both formal and informal occasions.

Rhodes, Cecil John (1853-1902) - Financier, industrialist, politician, and diplomat who made a fortune in gold and diamond mining. Born in England, he moved to Africa in 1870, helping colonize the nation later named for him, Southern Rhodesia, today known as Zimbabwe. He endowed fellowships for British and American students to attend Oxford University. Rhodes University in South Africa is named after him. Rhodes was committed to expanding British colonialism.

Rhodesia - See **Zimbabwe**.

Rhodies - A term coined by Rhodesian whites to refer to themselves as superior to the majority black population. The term developed sometime during the period of 1965 to 1979. In 1965, whites declared an end to the British colony of Southern Rhodesia, which has been named after Cecil Rhodes. They founded a new nation they called Rhodesia, and they excluded blacks from participating in economic, social, and political power. Since independence in 1980, the term Rhodies has become a pejorative label applying to whites in Zimbabwe who are nostalgic for the days when whites ruled, before black rebel groups rose up against them and declared liberation.

savanna - A plain with few trees and mainly coarse grasses. These plains are found in subtropical and tropical regions where rainfall is seasonal.

Salisbury - See **Harare**.

Shaka Zulu - One of the most powerful kings of the Zulu Kingdom. He brought many Northern Nguni peoples into the Zulu Kingdom, which under his leadership controlled Southern Africa between the Phongolo and Mzimkhulu Rivers. He has been called both a military genius and a brutal tyrant.

shekere - A West African instrument made from a dried gourd with beads woven into a net covering the gourd. Throughout Africa, there are similar gourd/bead or gourd/seed percussion instruments.

Shona (or Mashona) - An ethnic group belonging to the Bantu peoples in Southern Africa, who share a common Shona culture and language. This group constitutes more than two-thirds of the population of Zimbabwe.

Southern Rhodesia - See **Zimbabwe.**

Veld - An elevated open grassland, prairie, or steppe in Southern Africa covered with low shrubs and grasses. Veld comes from the Dutch word for "field."

Victoria Falls - A town in Matabeleland North, a province in the western part of Zimbabwe. Located on the southern bank of the Zambezi River, the town has a population of about 750,000. In 1900, British colonialists led by Cecil Rhodes settled in and gave the same name to the town near the spectacular waterfalls. By 1905, they had erected the Victoria Falls Bridge and built roads and railroads, joining the town with the cities of Hwange and Bulawayo and linking Zimbabwe with the country known today as Zambia. The waterfalls and the town attracted Western tourists, particularly between the 1930s and the 1960s and from the 1980s to the early 1990s. The Zimbabwe expression for Victoria Falls is Mosi oa-Tunya ("the smoke that thunders").

War Veterans - An informal way to refer to the Zimbabwe National Liberation War Veterans Association (ZNLWVA). The group is supposedly composed of former soldiers who fought during the Rhodesian Bush War on the side of the Zimbabwe African National Liberation Army (ZANLA) and the Zimbabwe People's Revolutionary Army (ZIPRA) against white Rhodesians' domination of the government. After the white rulers were deposed in 1980, the new government formed the ZNLWVA as a way to help the veterans assimilate back into civilian life, but the group had virtually no political power. In 1997, Chenjerai Hunzvi assumed its leadership, using the group to criticize President Mugabe's party, ZANU-PF. The veterans had been promised bonuses and support payments to reward their service, but had received small amounts. The economic downturn in the 1990s worsened their situation. Under Hunzvi, they demonstrated in Harare, winning bigger bonuses and payments from Mugabe's government. In 2000, a new demand appeared. The ZNLWVA wrote to Queen Elizabeth II, complaining that the majority of veterans were landless while most of Zimbabwe's lands were owned by descendants of British colonists, and threatening violence. Soon after, ZNLWVA members like Joseph Chinotimba led violent attacks on white-owned farms. It is assumed that Mugabe sanctioned these invasions. Although a war veteran usually led each attack, the invaders were far too young to have fought in the war. In 2005, the government began officially assimilating these youths into the army of Zimbabwe.

zaffer - a blue pigment used in ceramic glazes containing impure cobalt oxide.

Zaire (Republic of Zaire; since 1997, Democratic Republic of the Congo) - The name of a nation in Central Africa between 1971 and 1997. Before that, the region had been part of the Belgium Congo. Some Portuguese had named it Zaire after the Kongo word *nzere/nzadi* ("river that swallows all rivers"), as a reference to the Congo River. Although in 1960 the area won independence from colonial rule, in 1965, Mobutu Sese Seko led a coup and established a military dictatorship. He undertook a brutal campaign to eliminate colonial influences.

Zambezi River - A river in Central and Southern Africa, which begins in Northwest Zambia and flows through Southeast Zambia into Mozambique and to the Indian Ocean. It is the fourth-longest river in Africa (1,700 mi; 2,740 km).

zareba - In Northeast and Southeast Africa, a reference to an enclosure of thorny bushes or stakes protecting a village or campsite. The term can also refer to the village or campsite that is protected by this type of an enclosure.

Zimbabwe (formerly, Rhodesia and Southern Rhodesia) - A nation in Southern Africa. The earliest peoples inhabiting the region were the San, who in the first millennium were displaced by the Bantu. The Bantu consist of up to 600 ethnic groups from Central Africa down to Southeastern and Southern Africa who speak more than 500 Bantu languages. In the 1300s and 1400s, Bantu kingdoms emerged around water sources like the Great Lakes. For example, on the Zambezi River, the complex known as the Great Zimbabwe was erected. In the 7th century, Arabs arrived in Africa; by the 18th century, they were obtaining large numbers of slaves from Southeastern Africa. Likewise, Westerners were engaged in the slave trade. The arrival of the European colonists caused decline in Arab power in the region. European nations claimed various parts of Africa. From 1885 through World War I, Western occupation in Africa grew. Colonization of Zimbabwe began under the British South Africa Company founded by Cecil Rhodes, who arrived in Africa in 1870. Initially, the area was called South Zambezia, after the Zambezi River. The name Rhodesia came into use in 1895. Rhodes got mineral rights through treaties with indigenous leaders, and Queen Victoria chartered his company in 1889. He led British forces to conquer the Shona and Ndebele in establishing what would become the capital, Salisbury (now, Harare). The colony was renamed Southern Rhodesia in 1898, a name that lasted—through the establishment of self-governance in 1923—until 1964, when whites revolting against British rule changed it back to Rhodesia. The whites were defeated by black rebels in 1979, and the Republic of Zimbabwe was founded in 1980.

Zimbabwe African National Union-Patriotic Front (ZANU-PF) – See **Mugabe**.

Zulu - An ethnic group belonging to the Bantu peoples in Southern Africa, who share a common Zulu culture and language. Today, the nation of South Africa has the most Zulu, more than ten million, with smaller numbers living in Zimbabwe, Zambia, Tanzania, and Mozambique. During the 19th century, the Zulu king and warrior Shaka Zulu wielded control over large parts of Southern Africa.

ABOUT THE AUTHOR

Kathryn Waddell Takara, PhD, is the author of seven books. She is also a 2010 winner of the American Book Award (Before Columbus Foundation). She is a performance poet whose extensive travels in the United States, Africa, Europe, Central America, Tahiti, and China are often reflected in her writing.

She has previously published the book *Frank Marshall Davis: The Fire and the Phoenix (A Critical Biography)*—Davis was a journalist, poet, and labor activist of the Chicago Renaissance, cultural mentor of (Barry) President Barack Obama, author, and Takara's friend. She has also published *Timmy Turtle Teaches*, a colorful children's travel book. Her other publications include four books of poetry: from Ishmael Reed Press *New and Collected Poems*, and from Pacific Raven Press *Pacific Raven: Hawai`i Poems, Tourmalines: Beyond the Ebony Portal*, and *Love's Seasons: Generations Genetics Myths*. She has also published a collection of oral histories with African Americans in Hawai`i, scholarly articles, and more than 300 poems.

Born and raised in Tuskegee, Alabama, Takara is a retired Associate Professor from the University of Hawai`i at Mānoa, where she developed and taught courses in African American and African politics, history, literature, and culture. She has also taught French. Since retirement in 2007, she is the president and editor of Pacific Raven Press. Takara earned her PhD in Political Science and MA in French and has taught, advised, and mentored many individuals. She has appeared in a number of television programs and documentary films, and has given frequent interviews to publications and the media. She particularly enjoys her family and friends, pets, meditation, qigong, travel, reading and research, gardening, raising orchids, and interior design.

www.kathrynwaddelltakara.com
www.pacificravenpress.co

A portion of the proceeds from the sale of this book will be donated to The United Negro College Fund. The UNCF is the nation's largest and most effective minority education organization.